709

Company's Coming

A Spiritual Process for Creating More Welcoming Parishes

Dr. Richard J. McCorry

iUniverse, Inc.
New York   Bloomington

Company's Coming
A Spritual Process for Creating More Welcoming Parishes

Copyright © 2008 by Dr. Richard J. McCorry

iUniverse books may be ordered through booksellers or by contacting:

iUniverse
1663 Liberty Drive
Bloomington, IN 47403
www.iuniverse.com
1-800-Authors (1-800-288-4677)

ISBN: 978-0-595-52523-2 (pbk)
ISBN: 978-0-595-62576-5 (ebk)

Printed in the United States of America

To my son, Shawn McCorry

A fine man in whom I am most proud!

Table of Contents

Acknowledgments ix
Introduction 1
    Scriptural Basis 2
    Early Church History 3
    Modern Practice and the Call of Our Bishops 3
    Motivation 5
Becoming a Welcoming Parish Process - Overview 7
Assemble and Train a Parish Team 9
    Tips for Effective Presentations 10
Develop a Communications Plan 13
Assess Current Reality 15
    Methodology 15
    Observations 16
    Survey 16
        Mail Surveys 16
        Surveys Administered During Weekend Masses 18
        Survey Analysis 18
    Individual Interviews 19
Discern God's Vision 21
    Team Process 22
    Parish Community Process 22
Develop a Plan for Bringing the Ideal and Reality into Alignment 25
    Ushers vs. Greeters 26
Implement the Plan and Continuous Improvement 27
Appendix #1: Training Parish Welcoming Teams - Presentation
    Outline & Notes 29
Appendix #2: Practicing Catholic Hospitality - Handout 37
    Welcoming Parish Survey 42
    Observation worksheet 44
    Best Practices in Church Welcoming Programs 46
Church Welcoming Program -Selected Bibliography 51
About the Author 55
About The Center for Parish Hospitality 57

Acknowledgments

I wish to thank Bishop Frank Caggiano of the Roman Catholic Diocese of Brooklyn. Without his support, prayers and encouragement this book might never have been written. It was through his foresighted leadership that a pilot project utilizing this method was conducted in the Diocese of Brooklyn.

The Brooklyn Diocesan pilot project team was Robert Choiniere, director of pastoral planning, Deacon Rich Gilligan, assistant director of the Sts. Peter & Paul Spirituality Center, and Ellen Rhatigan, assistant director of pastoral planning. I am deeply indebted to them for their valuable guidance and advice which helped to form this program.

Fathers Peter Gillian, Ed Doran, Daniel Murphy, Michael Perry and Msgr. Guy Massie were the pastors of the five Brooklyn parishes which agreed to act as the "laboratory" in which this process was tested. It was through their enthusiastic embracing of a parish process to welcome the strangers among us that this project succeeded.

I am so grateful for the many dedicated parishioners of Corpus Christi, St. Gerard Majella, St. Saviour, and Our Lady of Refuge, all of the Brooklyn Diocese, who donated countless hours to employ this process so that their communities would truly reflect the hospitality that Christ modeled in His ministry.

Last, but certainly not least, I wish to thank Abbot John Denburger and the monks of the Abbey of the Genesee for their prayers and guidance offered on creating more hospitable parishes.

"The biggest disease is not leprosy or tuberculosis, But rather the feeling of being unwanted."

- Blessed Mother Theresa

Introduction

As Catholics, we have been challenged by the Lord to love our enemies (Mt 5:44). So, if we are called to love our enemies, certainly we are expected to love those who sit next to us in church. Right? And yet, how many times have newcomers to a church been greeted with a dirty look because they were sitting in someone else's seat?! An even more common experience is that visitors feel invisible, like their presence makes absolutely no difference to anyone. At the other end of the spectrum, how many times have newcomers been greeted warmly and made to feel welcomed? Sadly, there are many more experiences of the former than of the later.

In April, 2008 almost 1200 priests, deacons, vowed religious and lay ministers took part in a national summit to discuss the findings of the Emerging Models of Pastoral Leadership Project. This project identified one of the key marks of excellent parishes is that they are welcoming communities. At the same time, pastoral leaders surveyed by the same Emerging Models Project reported that this mark of excellence was the one at which they were least successful.[1] This book is intended to support pastoral leaders in developing a comprehensive program for creating more welcoming parishes.

Rarely have newcomers experienced Catholic churches as places where they are welcomed. Perhaps one of the reasons why we have not been more welcoming is because we have never had to worry about numbers of parishioners as necessary for our survival. And yet, it has been claimed that if former Catholics were a denomination unto themselves, that they would comprise the second largest denomination in the US (after current Catholics). Some leave the church and do not go to any church. But many are welcomed into upstart non-denominational Christian communities, and are greeted so warmly, that they never look back. This does not happen by accident, but is part of a very well thought out and executed plan. There

---

1.   Jewell, Marti. Keynote Address: Major Findings of the Emerging Models Project, April 21, 2008, pg. 5.

is much that we can learn from upstart Christian churches in terms of deliberately and intentionally welcoming the stranger.

If you asked committed members of a parish, they would undoubtedly say, "We want to be a welcoming place." But most parishes have never thought about, talked about or planned how this will happen. Generally speaking, once people get to know a newcomer in the Catholic Church, they do warm up and become welcoming. But as Christ said, "if you only love those who love you, what credit is that to you? For even sinners love those who love them," (Lk 6:32).

When new people come into a church, most decide in the first five minutes if they will ever come back. For this reason alone, it is important to be a welcoming parish. And this is especially true during this time in the church, as parishes are merging and consolidating. To have one's church closed is traumatic enough without having that trauma compounded by being made to feel invisible or outright unwelcomed in the new parish. A multitude of good works done by church leadership to heal the pain of a church closure can be undone quickly with one dirty look, for whatever reason, in the new parish.

A cursory review of Scripture and our religious tradition gives us the foundation upon which parish hospitality is grounded.

Scriptural Basis

Hospitality is manifested in an open and welcoming spirit; a willingness to drop what we are doing and receive the other person when they need us. We are reminded of Abraham and Sarah's hospitality to the three strangers (Gen 18:1-10). In welcoming the strangers, they were welcoming God. If we wish to grow in hospitality, we would do well to emulate the example of Abraham and Sarah.

The type of radical hospitality to which God calls us, requires that we give to the last measure. In Elijah's encounter with the widow of Zerephath, the widow gives out of the last of her food to the prophet, feeding him even before she feeds herself and her son. This radical hospitality requires not only generosity but also a good measure of faith. In return for her munificence, she is given enough food to last throughout the days of Israel's famine (1 Kings 17:7-16).

We recall Jesus' words: "what you do to the least of my brothers and sisters you do to me" (Mt 25:40). Christ gave us the exquisite example of hospitality at the last supper when he got on his knees and washed the disciples' feet (Jn

13:3-17). And he commanded us, who would claim to be his followers, to do likewise. If we really took this command seriously, we should be tripping over each other as we approached the strangers in our churches trying to make them feel welcomed. Jesus went on to say that we would ultimately be judged by God, in part, on the basis of the hospitality we extend to strangers; "for I was a stranger and you welcomed me," (Mt 25:35).

The nascent Christian community reflected the value of hospitality rooted in the Hebrew Scriptures and reaffirmed by Christ. Peter instructed his community to "be hospitable toward one another without complaining," (1 Pet 4:9). In the letter to the Romans, Paul told the community to, "extend hospitality to strangers," (Rom 12:13). Throughout all of Scripture hospitality is portrayed as a command from God, our duty toward others, and a clear path toward spiritual growth for ourselves.

Early Church History

In the early church, some of the faithful retreated to the desert to live a life of solitude, prayer, fasting and meditation as a path to grow closer to God. And yet, Thomas Merton writes that hospitality trumped all other spiritual practices. These fourth century desert Fathers would cheerfully break their fast and prayer to graciously receive guests.[2]

In the sixth century, St. Benedict codified this practice by writing rules for ordinary people wishing to live a Catholic life. These rules are still practiced by most monastic communities today. Chapter #53 of the rule states, "All guests who present themselves are to be welcomed as Christ."

Modern Practice and the Call of Our Bishops

Hospitality is still firmly rooted in modern monastic practice. The Catholic Worker Movement, founded in the United States during the height of the depression, practices radical hospitality rooted in our rich tradition of welcoming the stranger as we would receive Christ himself.

In 1999 the United States Conference of Catholic Bishops (USCCB) issued *Our Hearts Were Burning Within Us; A Pastoral Plan for Adult Faith Formation in the United States.* In it they stated, "To grow in discipleship throughout life, all believers need and are called to build vibrant parish

---

2.   Merton, Thomas, Wisdom of the Desert. New Direction Books, 1960

and diocesan communities of faith and service."[3] The process described in this book answers the call of that letter, in part, since it is envisioned that a good parish plan will include a strategy for catechizing the entire parish community into the call of the Gospel to treat the stranger as we would treat Christ.

The mandate to live hospitality is inextricably linked with the call of evangelization, to spread the good news of Jesus Christ to the entire world. It is converting in the fullest sense of that term; it will assist the ongoing conversion of existing parishioners by helping them to recognize and appreciate God's munificent hospitality toward us throughout history.[4] The church reflects this Good News when it behaves as Christ told us God will act toward us, as a loving, compassionate host. And when parishioners practice hospitality toward the newcomer they can become vehicles of conversion for others.

Practicing hospitality can also be a response to the call of stewardship in a number of ways. The 2002 USCCB document, *Stewardship; A Disciple's Response*, states, "Mature disciples make a conscious, firm decision, carried out in action, to be followers of Jesus Christ no matter the cost to themselves."[5] When parishioners practice hospitality, they are living out, in part, the call of stewardship. Furthermore, those who practice their faith in a truly welcoming environment are more likely follow that up with their financial support.

Finally, the 2000 USCCB pastoral letter, *Welcoming the Stranger Among Us: Unity in Diversity*, reminds us that as disciples of Christ we are required to establish and maintain a hospitable environment for all.[6] The process outlined in this book gives pastoral leaders a clear path towards establishing a welcoming parish community.

---

3. USCCB, Our Hearts Were Burning Within Us; A Pastoral Plan for Adult Faith Formation in the United States. November, 1999, #3.

4. USCCB, Go and Make Disclple:. A National Plan and Strategy for Catholic Evangelization in the United States.
November, 1992.

5. USCCB, Stewardship A Disciple's Response. 10th Anniversary Edition, 2002, p. 5.

6. USCCB, Welcoming the Stranger Among Us: Unity in Diversity. 2000.

Motivation

Scripture tells us that those who practice hospitality will be rewarded by God. Abraham and Sarah received the reward of a child from God for their hospitality. The widow and her son were rewarded by God for sharing the last of their meager rations with Elijah. But receiving a reward should not be our motivation.

Our parishes will grow and thrive when we practice hospitality. With increased numbers of parishioners our collections will grow and we will have more people available to contribute their time and talent toward parish ministries. More hands make light work. But we should not practice hospitality for these reasons.

Individually, parishioners will feel greater commitment to a parish that is welcoming and will be more inclined to invite their friends and neighbors to a parish where they know their friends will be received warmly. People will be more encouraged to actively participate in the liturgy when they feel welcomed. But this still should not be our motivation.

Our motivation for becoming more welcoming communities and people needs to spring out of the awareness that this is God's fervent wish for us. Spiritually mature people are well aware of God's manifold gifts freely given to them, and gratitude springs out of this awareness. It is with this sense of overwhelming gratitude that faith filled people desire to carry out God's commands and wishes. That God desires us to welcome the stranger is reinforced many times over in the Hebrew Scripture, the teachings of Christ, and the various Epistles. Living the virtue of hospitality should be its own reward, and any ancillary benefits should be seen as additional gifts from God, something which is neither desired nor earned. Wherever hospitality is practiced out of gratitude, the face of a loving, accepting God is made manifest, appealing to those yearning for a faith community that they can call home. Creating a culture of hospitality in today's parishes will require extensive catechesis, deliberate planning and careful implementation. This should be the goal of any good parish plan for creating more welcoming communities.

Becoming a Welcoming Parish Process - Overview

Becoming a welcoming parish is a process, not an event. Since the circumstances of each parish in unique, there is no "one size, fits all" plan for growing into a welcoming parish. What follows is one possible spiritual process, rooted in solid organizational planning principles, which a parish can employ to develop and implement a strategy to become a more welcoming community. What follows are suggestions which need to be adapted to the lived circumstances of individual parishes.

Ideally, this process must come out of the felt need of the pastor to transform his parish into a more welcoming community. Parishes have a hard time transcending the limitations of their pastor, so without the pastor's active support, the potential success of this process is greatly restricted, perhaps impossible.

The basic steps to this process are:
1. Assemble and train a parish team.
2. Develop a communication plan.
3. Assess current reality.
4. Discern God's vision.
5. Develop a plan for bringing God's vision and reality into alignment.
6. Implement the plan, measure the results and continuous improvement.

Assemble and Train a Parish Team

The pastor, or his designee, needs to assemble a team, composed primarily of parishioners, with appropriate staff support. Bulletin articles and announcements at the end of Mass can be used to recruit team members, but the pastor could also personally invite influential, active members of the parish that he believes would be well suited for this team. Team members need to be informed of the substantial commitment of time required by this process. Ideally, the team size should be between 8-14 members.

This team will be divided into three subcommittees: assessment, communications, and implementation, according to the desires and skills of team members. It will be the responsibility of the assessment subcommittee to conduct and/or oversee the assessment of reality stage of this process. The communications subcommittee will be tasked with the very important assignment of keeping the rest of the parish informed of this effort and its progress. Lastly, the implementation subcommittee will conduct and/or oversee the implementation of the plan developed by the entire team.

Once the team members have been identified and recruited, a day of prayer and reflection should be scheduled for the team. The goals for this day are:

1. To sensitize team members to the importance of becoming a welcoming community and to the personal and spiritual needs of strangers when they first walk through the door.

2. To meditate upon the examples and commands of Scripture and recent church documents in regards to welcoming the stranger.

3. To decide upon the decision making process that the team will employ.

4. To acquaint the team members with an outline of this process and begin to delegate tasks and responsibilities.

5. To motivate and begin to instill a sense of team in its members.

6. To begin to discern God's will for the welcoming program of this parish.

This training should be done by someone who has skills in public presentations, facilitating group discussions, and in multimedia presentations. Additionally, the presenter should be well versed in this process, in the scriptural basis for hospitality, and in our rich tradition of welcoming the stranger. The Center for Parish Hospitality would be happy to provide a presenter with all the above skills, for your parish team training. For further information, please refer to the web site at: www.catholichospitality.com/serv03.htm.

Tips for Effective Presentations

The best presentations are those that are tailored to the needs of the particular audience you will be addressing. This requires consultation with someone who knows the group and the circumstances they are experiencing, most likely the pastor or other person making the request for the presentation.

Consider molding the presentation around the acronym of 'LEAP.' These four components, although not presented in this order, are:
1. Learning
2. Experiential
3. Action
4. Prayer

By design, there is a learning component to these presentations. Participant will be presented with new material which must be explained.

Confucius said, "tell me something and I'll probably forget it, show me something and I may remember, help me to experience it and I'll have it for life." Since most of the struggles people have around change transpire on the feelings level, by far the largest component of these reflection sessions should be experiential, both individually and in small groups. Creating more welcoming communities will require, in most cases, a change of belief and practice. In terms of the individual experiential component, participants are given handouts that contained questions which will help participants identify issues and feelings they are having around this particular change.

In order to establish the ground rules for the small group work, people are asked to honor the confidentiality of that which people will share. Furthermore, participants are instructed that when they brake into their small groups, they are to listen to what the others share and not to offer advice or feedback. People should be informed ahead of time that they will be asked to share their responses in small groups. This is based upon feedback from participants in earlier reflection sessions that they had initially chosen a very personal issue and then had to scramble for something less personal when informed that they would be sharing this in small groups.

The prayer component should be woven throughout the presentation. After the introduction of the presenters and participants, there is an opening prayer, inviting the Holy Spirit to guide the participants during the training session. The session should also close with prayer.

Finally, the action component of the reflection session is the charge given to participants. They should be commissioned to put into action the concepts and strategies presented at the reflection session. Furthermore, they are encouraged to go out and share this material with someone else within the next 24 hours. This will help to solidify the material in their own mind. Finally, participants should be instructed to attend a worship service at another church, Catholic or otherwise, where they have never been before and where they are not known. Using the observation worksheet contained in the handout material (Appendix #2) they should reflect on the experience of being a newcomer in that faith community.

Fully half of the total time of the training reflection session is devoted to the experiential and prayerful components of the reflection session. This is intentionally done so that the Holy Spirit might have ample time to touch the hearts of the participants to let them know that no matter what, they will never be left alone as they struggle through the changes that are required of them. Nevertheless, in spite of such assurances, the participants, and all people facing change, must ultimately take a LEAP of faith, trusting that our loving God will give us all we need to adapt and adapt well to the changes ahead for our church.

Some additional practical tips:

1. We are living in hyper stimulated times. Lecture alone is deadly boring and rarely communicates the message you're trying to get across. Your presentation should be supported by audio/visuals with generous amounts of audience participation.

2. Always have a backup plan! Murphy's Law is always operative with audio/visual presentations. Slideshows can be converted into a movie and burned onto a DVD. If a DVD is going to be shown, have a backup player. Ideally, the presenter should have his/her own projector and lap top computer. Relying upon the group to provide a projector or laptop is fraught with difficulties.

3. Get to the presentation location well ahead of time, set up all the audio/visual equipment and run through the presentation to make sure everything is working.

4. Practicing the presentation ahead of time will add to its polished appearance and your own confidence. Practicing before a video camera and critiquing it afterward with someone else is ideal.

5. Its good to have water available during your talk, in case your mouth gets dry. It is a bad practice, however, to have that water near your computer or any other electrical equipment.

6. Early on in the presentation, check with the participants to make sure they can hear you.

7. Real life stories which help to illustrate a point are like gold.

8. Humor, if you have the gift, helps keep an audience engaged. If you don't have the gift, it is just annoying. If you're not sure if you're funny, you're probably not. Ask someone who will be honest with you.

9. Be animated as you present your material, move around somewhat, even if you must remain in the area of the podium, microphone or projector.

10. Design an opening that will capture and hold the audience's attention.

11. Tell them what you are going to tell them, tell it to them, then tell them what you told them. People need repetition to break through the psychological mechanism we all have for filtering out information.

12. Mahatma Gandhi said that we must become the change we want to bring about in the world. Therefore, this training and reflection session should be a model of hospitality.

Five hours should be sufficient for this training, including a lunch break. Done in a daylong format, these workshops could be held on either Saturdays or Sundays. Alternatively, if a parish wished, this training could be done on two consecutive week nights from 7PM-9PM.

Appendix #1 is a presentation outline and presenter's notes for training parish teams. Appendix #2 is a portion of the handout material that would be distributed to the parish team members at the training.

Develop a Communications Plan

The surest way to hinder any parish welcoming effort is to leave it exclusively in the hands of a small committee. The ultimate success of any welcoming program will hinge upon the engagement of the entire parish. They need to be informed, educated, and motivated through the communication plan. Therefore, this process needs to be transparent and engaging for the rest of the parish and this is done through early and repeated communications utilizing a variety of media. It will be this communication effort that will motivate the rest of the parish and provide them with the necessary information to hopefully create a uniformly welcoming environment in the parish. Communication about such change requires more than just one sermon and/or a bulletin article. The communication strategy needs to be written and specific. A sub-committee of the parish team will be identified during the day of prayer and training whose task it will be to devise and implement the communications plan throughout the unfolding of this process.

What needs to be communicated? Short answer - Everything! To whom? Everyone. Certainly, the vision needs to be communicated. Under communicating the vision is one of the major causes of a plan failing. And it is God's vision that is communicated, not the committee's vision.

The current assessment of reality needs to be communicated as well; people need to know the reason(s) behind any proposed change. The distance that exists between God's vision and the current reality establishes creative tension, the type of tension that creates motivation for change.

Once the plan is developed, this can be communicated to the parish. While the plan is being implemented, status updates can be given to the parish community.

There are several matters that must be considered when developing a communication strategy. First, the appropriate pace - the rate at which people can absorb new information. Second, the different learning styles that exist in a parish community. Third, most people have a built in filter which screens out new information. Therefore, the communication needs to be repeated and offered through various modalities. The communication strategy should be creative. The communication subcommittee might consider: small group discussion, youth group drama, appropriate music, special newsletter(s), video, web site, developing a unique vocabulary that has special meaning for your parish, and repeat, repeat, repeat.

Communication subcommittee members should seek feedback from others to see if the communication is getting through. Finally, the communication strategy should respond, in a public way, to all questions and concerns that people have expressed.

Assess Current Reality

One of the necessary ingredients in any change initiative is creative tension. Groups will rarely find the motivation to change without this essential element. The simplest way for church leaders to generate creative tension is to discern the ideal and compare it with an accurate assessment of reality. Therefore, this assessment seeks to discern the current reality of the parish in terms of how it actually welcomes newcomers. It is further designed to determine how the parishioners evaluate the welcoming of the parish as well as the importance they give to welcoming the newcomer. It is also hoped that the parish team might get a glimpse of God's will for this community through this assessment, since God's will is revealed, in part, through the community of believers.

This assessment of reality should be done before the discernment of God's vision, since discerning God's vision ahead could influence the assessment of reality by causing people to respond to questions with answers that are not based in reality but according to an idealized goal which has little resemblance to the facts.

Methodology

There are three main components to this assessment. The first component is that an observer, new to the community, attends all the weekend Masses, and reports on the experience s/he had as a newcomer. The second component is a 34 question survey that is administered to active parishioners. Lastly, a handful of active parishioners are interviewed either in person or by phone. It will be the responsibility of the assessment subcommittee, working in concert with the necessary staff support to accomplish this important step in the process.

Observations

The purpose of the observations is to place a stranger in the community and observe three key areas of welcoming: the facility, the bulletin (and web site, if any), and specific worship experiences. It is suggested that the assessment subcommittee recruit someone from another parish to attend all the weekend celebration of the Eucharist and report back to the committee in written form. A suggested observation worksheet, which can guide the observer's work, are the last two pages of Appendix #2. If the assessment subcommittee would prefer, The Center for Parish Hospitality can provide a trained observer to attend the weekend Masses and issue the subcommittee a comprehensive written report. The Center's web site contains a sample report at www.catholichospitality.com/resources.htm.

Survey

This survey is designed to learn two primary factors affecting hospitality: 1) the extent to which parishioners see this as a welcoming community and 2) the extent to which parishioners value a welcoming parish community. Parishioners are also asked in this survey for any suggestions they may have for creating a more welcoming community as well as whether they would like to be involved in a parish hospitality effort. It is also hoped that the team can get a glimpse of God's will for the parish through this survey, since one of the ways God speaks is through the community of believers.

Appendix #2 contains a sample survey that could be used. The survey results for parishioners should be evaluated separately from the survey results for staff and key leadership people in the parish. This will show if there is any significant disconnect between the parishioner's view and the view of those in parish leadership.

There are two possible methods for administering the survey: by sending out the surveys in the mail to active parishioners or by having parishioners complete the survey during the weekend Masses.

Mail Surveys

The following are some guidelines regarding the sending out of these surveys:

1. To get as good a sampling as possible, distribute a minimum of 300 total surveys. Try to insure that they're sent to parishioners who regularly

attend Mass. Perhaps a computerized record is kept of those regularly depositing envelopes in the collection to facilitate this identification.

2. For those surveys sent through the mail, please include a self-addressed, stamped envelope for ease of reply. A suggested cover letter from the pastor follows these instructions.

3. Encourage people through bulletin articles and Mass announcements to return the completed surveys. Publicize ahead of time that the surveys are going out and then follow up the weekend after they are distributed. Continue asking for the surveys to be returned until you have received back at least 150 completed surveys. These announcements (bulletin and pulpit) are also an opportunity to begin sensitizing the parish to the importance of becoming a more welcoming community and how this has been identified as a felt need for your parish. While much more labor intensive, this method would be preferable if a pastor did not want to encumber the Sunday celebration of the Eucharist with people filling out a survey.

Suggested Survey Cover Letter

My dear sisters and brothers in Christ, (personalized letters are even better, albeit more labor intensive)

As Catholics, we have been challenged by the Lord to love our enemies (Mt 5:44). So, if we are called to love our enemies, certainly we are expected to love those who sit next to us in church. Right? It is because hospitality is so important, especially in our very mobile culture that the parish is embarking on a process to make it more welcoming to newcomers.

As part of that process, we have to get a clear picture of the current reality and this is how you can help. Enclosed please find a survey that should only take about 10 minutes to complete. Please do complete this survey today and drop it back in the mail to us, using the enclosed self addressed stamped envelope. Please don't set it aside to do later but complete it now.

It is important that you answer the survey honestly, reporting how the situation really is, rather than how it should be. May God continue to bless you for your generosity and commitment to this parish!

Yours in Christ,

Pastor

Surveys Administered During Weekend Masses

It is a much simpler matter to ask people to complete the surveys during weekend celebrations of the Mass. Some pastors choose to do this during homily time, others after the reception of Communion. This method helps to insure that the survey is administered to active parishioners and eliminates the time and expense of mailing.

Survey Analysis

Ideally, the parish will have a member who is skilled in statistical analysis to process the results of the surveys. The Center for Parish Hospitality can also process the surveys and issue a comprehensive report to the assessment subcommittee. The Center's web site contains a sample survey analysis report at www.catholichospitality.com/resources.htm.

Any good analysis of the surveys should contain the following information:

1. Description of the sample size: How many surveys were analyzed?

2. Description of survey respondents: males vs. females, range of years the respondents were parish members, range of ages of the respondents, and marital status.

3. Specific statement responses: how many respondents answered 1, 2, 3, 4, or 5 to each question? What percentage of respondents answered 1, 2, 3, 4, or 5 to each question? What was the average response to each question (expressed as a decimal to the hundredth place)?

4. Establish a composite score: determine and compare the average response for each of the two categories of questions (How is our church doing vs. How important this is to you)? How many respondents felt the parish was doing a better job of welcoming than the importance they personally felt for welcoming the newcomers? How many respondents felt the parish was doing a worse job of welcoming than the importance they personally felt for welcoming the newcomers? How many respondents felt the parish was doing exactly the type of job of welcoming as the importance they personally felt for welcoming the newcomers?

5. Compare and contrast the composite score for new parishioners (those that identified themselves as members of the parish for five years or less) vs. those who identified themselves as parishioners for more than five years.

6. Compare and contrast the composite score for parishioners 30 years of age or younger vs. those over 30 years of age.

7. New member demographics: describe those respondents who identified themselves as parishioners for five years or less (gender, age, marital status).

8. The report should contain the names and contact information for all those who said they would like to be part of an effort to make new people feel welcomed.

9. Finally, the report should contain all the suggestions survey respondents wrote in for how the parish can become more welcoming.

Individual Interviews

The parish will identify a handful of active parish members willing to be interviewed in person or over the telephone. There are several reasons for conducting these interviews. The first reason is as a consistency check on the results of the parish written survey. Also, to determine the extent to which catechesis relative to welcoming the stranger might be needed in the parish community. Additionally, to elicit suggestions for how the parish could become a more welcoming community. Finally, like the surveys, it is also hoped that the parish team can get a glimpse of God's will for this parish in terms of welcoming the newcomer, since one of the ways God speaks is through the community of believers.

The following are suggested questions for these interviews:

1. How well does the parish welcome newcomers?

2. How important is welcoming newcomers to you.

3. Can you think of a story in the Bible which features welcoming the stranger or extending hospitality to a newcomer?

4. What would you see as the benefits, if any, for our parish becoming a more welcoming parish?

5. Ultimately who is responsible for our parish becoming a welcoming community?

6. Do you have any suggestions for how our parish can become a more welcoming community?

A summary of these interviews should be submitted in written form to the assessment subcommittee. The report should also contain a description of the respondents: age, gender, years a member of the parish, and marital status.

The results of the entire assessment of reality (observations, surveys, and individual interviews) should be communicated often, and in a variety of ways, to the entire parish community. This is the mechanism by which people will be invited into the creative tension that will hopefully create the motivation in many to change, become more aware and/or improve their behavior toward the strangers in their midst.

An example report of this three fold assessment can be found on The Center for Parish Hospitality web site at: www.catholichospitality.com/resources.htm.

Discern God's Vision

This planning process can only be effectively done in a prayerful environment, where the parish team believes that the Holy Spirit is active in their deliberations and prays for the gift of the Holy Spirit's perspective. The team, with the guidance of the pastor or his designee, attempts to discern God's vision for this parish with regards to welcoming the stranger. Attempting to discern God's vision raises the group's sight and helps to mediate self-centered motivations.

This vision should lift the parish out of the mundane; it should create a spark that impels the parish community to action. Some key questions that will guide this process are: For what purpose did God establish the church? What is God's specific call with regard to this parish and the way it welcomes the stranger? What is God's vision for the first experience a person has when they visit your church? What does God want them to feel? How would God help them to get over the universal awkwardness that people feel when they walk into a new situation?

The group can employ the following resources to discern God's vision:

1. Bible - are there specific passages in the Hebrew and Christian Scriptures that speak to God's vision for the community of believers with regard to welcoming the stranger? ie., Gen 18:1-10 & Jn 13:3-17.

2. Church documents - Are there Church documents that address how the church community is to welcome newcomers? ie., The 2000 USCCB report entitled, *Welcoming the Stranger Among Us; Unity in Diversity*.

3. Spiritual directors - taking these questions to a spiritual director and seeking guidance.

4. Seeking the guidance of other faith filled people. When we hear the same comments from several people who have not conversed then perhaps that is the Holy Spirit speaking through them.

5. Asking these key questions in prayer and listening for the answer.

6. Dreams

7. Above all else: prayer, prayer, and more prayer.

There are many different means by which the group can attempt to discern God's vision for the parish with regards to welcoming the stranger. Two possible processes are outlined below. The first process would involve the pastor (or his designee) and the entire parish team. The second process would involve the entire parish community. Either process can be adapted as the group and/or pastor sees fit.

Team Process

1. During the initial team training, the task of discerning God's vision will be explained and the process begun.

2. The team will go away from that training with the instruction to continue discerning God's will and to seek the input of others in this discernment while continuing to take it into personal prayer.

3. The team then comes together for group prayer, meditation and to write a first draft.

4. The team would then seek private feedback by asking these questions about the first draft: is it clear? Is it comprehensive? Is it compelling?

5. Out of this feedback would come a revise second draft.

6. The team would then obtain additional private feedback. There are four major questions the team needs to have answered about the revised second draft: What is overall reaction? Any questions about the meaning of the vision? Any ideas that need to be added or deleted? Are there ways to say this better?

7. A final meeting would be held where the team would obtain a group consensus (or whatever decision making style the team has chosen) about the final form of the vision statement. The team will then turn over the final vision statement to the communication subcommittee to publicize to the rest of the parish community according to the communication strategy.

Parish Community Process

This process is the same as above except that at step #6, the team would then obtain public feedback by holding a town hall type meeting, properly advertised to the entire parish. Again, there are four major questions the team needs to have answered in this public forum: What is overall reaction? Any questions about the meaning of the vision? Any ideas that need to be added or deleted? Are there ways to say this better?

Ghandi said that we must become the change we wish to bring about in the world. Therefore this gathering should be designed to model the type of hospitality the team wishes to bring about in the parish. Greeters at the door, people introducing themselves to those around them and providing refreshments are a few of the suggested hospitality steps to take at this gathering.

The benefit of the team only process is that it is more expedited and less complicated. If a team desired to expedite the process even further, one of the two revisions can be eliminated. The benefit of the parish community process is that it provides a forum for sensitizing the parish community to the need of being welcoming to the stranger while seeking their "buy in" to this entire initiative.

Develop a Plan for Bringing the Ideal and Reality into Alignment

The team should first attempt to come up with the ideal welcoming program without regard to what other parishes have done. After they have exhausted their own imaginations, they can then research successful welcoming programs employed by other parishes. The 2000 USCCB document, entitled, *Welcoming the Stranger Among Us; Unity in Diversity*, should be referred to during this stage in the process, and the committee should be guided by its observations and recommendations.

This overall approach will assist the group in "thinking outside of the box," on this very important issue. Appendix #2 contains a list of some best practices in programs designed to welcome newcomers into our churches.

The exact plan for bringing God's ideal vision and the current reality together will necessarily vary from parish to parish. Effective plans will address:

1. Ways to educate and motivate parishioners to value and welcome the stranger in their midst. The major forums for accomplishing this would include preaching at Mass and the weekly bulletin.

2. Creating multiple entry points for new people. Churches need metaphorical "side doors" through which people may enter into parish life. This could include small support groups, coffeehouses, even sports; all are paths through which new people can connect with established parishioners outside of the weekly celebration of the Mass.

3. Once new people are identified, mechanisms should be established to follow up with them: contact visitors, track attendance, and help people connect to the church family.

Ushers vs. Greeters

Most parishes have a dedicated group of people who act as ushers. At the same time, many of these ushers have developed such bad habits as: visiting amongst themselves when they should be greeting, overlooking unfamiliar people and only greeting those they know, organizing bulletins and collection baskets when they should be greeting those entering the church, distracting people by visiting during the liturgy and so forth. If the pastoral team truly believes that the current group of ushers can be molded into the types of greeters that the team desires, with a minimum of pushback from the ushers, then by all means they should pursue this strategy. Many parish teams, however, might decide that less energy will be expended by recruiting and forming a new group of parishioners who acts strictly as greeters rather than trying to change the behavior of existing ushers.

Implement the Plan and Continuous Improvement

Once a plan is established, the implementation subcommittee should begin overseeing its implementation. Each step toward implementation should be measured in some way to insure that the plan is having the desire effect. This measurement does not have to be as extensive as the initial assessment of reality, and could involve some well chosen personal interviews with both newcomers and established parishioners during the implementation. The measurement portion of the implementation would be the responsibility of the assessment subcommittee.

The team should be prepared to adjust the plan as issues arise during implementation. This is not to say that the plan should be jettisoned if it does not immediately change the status quo, but at the same time, the plan should not be slavishly followed when it is clear that it is not having the desired result.

At some point after the entire plan has been implemented for awhile, the same assessment of reality done prior to implementation (observation by a newcomer, survey, and individual interviews) should be conducted. The purpose of this second full assessment of reality is to see if the plan has had a positive, negative, or neutral impact on the welcoming of the parish, as well as the perceptions of parishioners as to the welcoming of the parish. Beyond that, limited measurement should be continuous, thereby monitoring the situation long after the plan has been fully implemented.

Appendix #1

TRAINING PARISH WELCOMING TEAMS
PRESENTATION OUTLINE & NOTES

Prior to the training:

    1. Purchase the video "What Visitors See," from the Church Growth Network, P.O. Box 892589, Temecula, CA 92589. 1 951-506-9086,
    2. Obtain an adequate amount of copies of the 2000 USCCB document, entitled, "Welcoming the Stranger Among Us; Unity in Diversity," for all of the team members.
    3. Obtain sufficient copies of this book to distribute to all team members.
    4. Make enough copies of the handout (appendix #2) to distribute to all team members.

    Materials needed:

    Pens and/or pencils
    1. A backpack filled with a number of books to give the backpack weight
    2. Several index cards with recent personal prayer request written on them, ie., "Please pray for my mom as she undergoes chemotherapy."
    3. A Bible
    4. Name tags
    5. Several pads of newsprint, markers, and easels, a sufficient number for small group work.

    Outline of Presentation

    Gathering Prayer

Read Phil. 2:3-4 - "Do nothing from selfish ambition or conceit, but in humility regard others as better than yourselves. Let each of you look not to your own interests, but to the interests of others."

Prayers of Petition (invite participants to offer spontaneous prayers plus add the following)[7]

For the gift of hospitality, so all arriving immigrants will be welcomed and treated with human dignity. We pray to the Lord.

Response: Lord, hear our prayer.

For migrants, refugees, and strangers in our midst, that they may find hope in our concern for justice and feel the warmth of our love, we pray to the Lord.

Response: Lord, hear our prayer.

Gathering all our prayers together, let us offer the prayer to the Father that Jesus taught us . . . Our Father . . .

Faith Sharing - point out faith sharing guidelines in the box on page 1 of the handout material then have people break into small groups of two or three and have them share for about ten minutes how the reading from Philippians speaks to their heart.

When the participants come back into the large group, ask if anyone would like to share their response from the small group. Then go around the room and ask people to identify themselves and what they hope to get out of this gathering.

1. Introduction

Hospitality is not optional and it is not safe. Spend just 30 minutes watching the news and you will know that we live in dangerous times. So we have good reason to be wary of the stranger. But following the way of Christ is not the way of the world.

---

7. From *Welcoming the Stranger Among Us; Unity in Diversity*, USCCB: 2000.

a) "You only have one chance to make a first impression" exercise: on handout have people write down the first word or thought that comes to mind for each category. Then have them share their responses in the large group. Ask people to describe any "wow" experiences they have had in any of these venues. Give an example yourself.

b) Ask - What is one of our primary purposes for existing as a church? Ultimately explain the great commission (Mt 28:19) - to carry the Gospel to all nations and how hospitality is necessary a part of that commission.

2. Discuss Hospitality:
    a) in the historic Semitic culture
    b) in the Hebrew and Christian Scriptures
        1) the example of Abraham (Genesis 18:1-5)
        2) the many examples of Jesus
    c) in the Semitic culture today

3. Discuss the relative merits of the terms: guest vs. visitor, host vs. greeter.

4. Ask the large group to brainstorm the benefits of making a good impression with guests: for the parish, for the guests, for the parishioners.

5. Ask the group to remember times when they have been guests then have them complete the following exercise.

Who Is Our Guest Exercise
Needs:
    - 4 to 6 recently submitted anonymous prayer requests on small cards or paper
    - a backpack weighted with several books
    - poster board or newsprint for each group
    - markers for each group

Refer participants to the questions in their handouts to direct their considerations. Break up the participants into small groups and allow 10-15 minutes for them to describe the typical guest to their parish. Have each group depict this guest in someway on poster board or newsprint.

Have groups report to the larger group their discernment of our guests. When they are done, pass around the backpack and have prayer requests in

31

a pocket of this backpack weighted down with books. Have each group take one prayer request and read it aloud.

When all the prayer requests have been read, explain that the backpack represents the burden each guest carries with them when they enter a new church. The prayers for relief are part of this burden as well. Ask the group to respond by a show of hands, "how many of you have entered a new church with burdens, concerns, questions, fears?" Most should raise their hands and thereby begin to identify with the newcomer.

Share demographic trends in the area to depict who the next guest might be. Additionally note:
- Faithful Catholics coming from a parish that has closed.
- Immigrants.
- Christmas & Easter Catholics.
- Christian's from other denominations.
- Unchurched.

6. Show the video, "What Visitors See," the ten moments of truth for guests to a church.

When you are a greeter you are the church. You may be the only Bible or catechism a person ever reads, so consider: what is it you'd like to communicate in your encounter with a guest? Better yet, what is it God would like you to communicate in your encounter with a guest?

Enter into a discussion about whether the purpose of church is to cater to every whim of its members, like you would to a guest. Surely not, but the point is that you have to get and hold people's attention before you can teach them. Practicing hospitality is one way of getting and holding new people's attention. Point out the example of Paul in the Areopagus (Acts 17:16-31).

7. Describe the Parish Process for Discerning and Implementing a Welcoming Program
    a. Identify and Form Parish Teams. These teams would be composed of prayerful people with a demonstrated commitment to the future of the Church.
        i. Determine decision making process: majority vote, consensus, unanimous, pastor decide.
        ii. Assign Tasks and choose subcommittees: Communications, assessment, implementation.

iii. Develop communication plan so that this process is transparent to the rest of the parish. The ultimate success of this program will rise or fall on the commitment of the rest of the parish. They need to be informed, educated, and motivated through the communication plan. Communicate early and often.

(1) What needs to be communicated? Short answer - Everything! To whom? Everyone.

(2) The vision - under communicating is one of the major causes of a plan failing.

(3)The current assessment of reality - people need to know the reason(s) behind any change proposed.

(4) The change plan.

(5) Status updates.

iv. Steps and considerations

(1) Pace - the rate at which people can absorb new information.

(2) Personality - different learning styles

(3) Develop an explicit communication strategy

(4) Be creative - communication about change requires more than just a sermon and bulletin article - consider:

    a. small group discussion

    b. youth group drama

    c. involve music ministry

    d. special newsletter(s) mailed to parishioners

    e. Create or show an appropriate video

    f. web site.

(5) develop a unique vocabulary which has special meaning for your parish.

(6) Answering publically questions that people ask in private.

(7) Repeat, repeat, repeat

v. Seek feedback to see if the communication is getting through.

b. Assess the current parish reality. Determine: 1) How welcoming is the parish? 2) how important is being a welcoming parish to parishioners?

a. Survey (sample in Appendix #2).

b. Observations

c. Individual Interviews

d. When completed, commit the assessment of the current reality to writing, as detailed as possible, and communicate to the rest of the parish.

c. Discern God's vision for the parish with regards to hospitality.

Ask: How do we go about discerning God's vision?

The group can employ the following resources to discern God's vision:

- Bible - are there specific passages in the Hebrew and Christian Scriptures that speak to God's vision for the community of believers with regard to welcoming the stranger? Ie., Gen 18:1-10 & Jn 13:3-17.

- Church documents - Are there Church documents which address how the church community is to welcome newcomers? ie., The 2000 USCCB report entitled, *Welcoming the Stranger Among Us; Unity in Diversity.*

- Spiritual directors - taking these questions to a spiritual director and seeking guidance.

- Seeking the guidance of other faith filled people. When we hear the same comments from several people who have not conversed then perhaps that is the Holy Spirit speak through them.

- Asking these key questions in prayer and listening for the answer.

- Above all else: prayer, prayer, prayer.

Engaging and beginning the process of discerning God's vision:

- Invite the Holy Spirit into all aspects of this discernment.

- Remind them that this is God's vision, not our own.

- Only limitation here is the imagination. Do not consider people, finances, or facilities yet.

Have someone read Matthew 25:31-40 out loud. Break into small groups and ask them to begin discerning God's vision for a welcoming parish community for 10 minutes.

Have groups report when you come back into the large group and have someone record the group's responses.

d. Develop a plan for moving the parish from the current reality to the ideal.

e. Implement the plan developed. Conduct spot measurement as the plan is implemented.

f. When plan is fully implemented, conduct another full assessment (as in c above) to determine if ideal has been achieved.

8. Closing Prayer

Read Jn 13:1-15 - Jesus washing the disciples' feet at the last supper.

9. Homework assignment – ask the participants to attend a Mass or religious service at a place that they have never attended before and where no one knows them before they attend the next team meeting. Refer them to the observation worksheet of the handout for a guide to conducting these observations.

Appendix #2

PRACTICING CATHOLIC HOSPITALITY - HANDOUT

Opening Prayer

Phil 2:3-4 - "Do nothing from selfish ambition or conceit, but in humility regard others as better than yourselves. Let each of you look not to your own interests, but to the interests of others."

Prayers of Petition (Feel free to offer your prayer requests)

Lord's Prayer

Faith Sharing - Take a moment to prayerfully reflect upon the reading from Paul's letter to the Philippians and after a couple of minutes move into groups of three when you're ready and share how this reading speaks to your heart. We'll take about ten minutes, so please limit your sharing time to about three minutes so everyone has a chance to share.

Faith Sharing Guidelines

✦ Share only that for which you feel comfortable. Consider before you share if you might feel uncomfortable later by what you are about to share.
✦ Members must respect confidentiality. Feel free to share and ideas or concepts that you have heard but please do not attribute any names to them.
✦ When we practice respect, charity, honesty, and openness we assist the spiritual growth of all.
✦ Participants need to feel comfortable with silence. It is that space in which the Holy Spirit works.
✦ Please allow sufficient time for all to share before sharing a second time.
✦ All are encouraged to share, both for their own benefit as well as the benfit of the group.

You Only Have One Chance to Make a First Impression

Write down the first word or thought that comes to mind for each item below.

Your Last Hotel Stay _____
Your Last Airline Experience _____
Your Bank _____
Your Local Church _____
McDonalds _____
Starbucks _____

Describe the Benefits of Making a Good Impression with Guests:

For the Parish:

For the Guest:

For the Host:

Who Is Our Guest?

Use the questions below as a launching pad for defining your parish's typical guest. Think of people such as your neighbors, friends, co workers, work partners, and the families of your children's friends. Decide how your group might illustrate your responses, creating as complete a "profile" as possible.

· What does this person do for a living?
· What "wow" experiences have they had in the past?
· What does he or she do for fun?
· Where does he or she shop? What persuades this person when shopping?
· Who are his or her friends? How deep are these friendships?
· How old is this person?
· Is this person married?

· Does this person attend school? Where? What's his or her focus?
· What about family? Does this person have children? If so, what schools do they attend?
· What are this person's goals and dreams?
· Why did he or she come to church last weekend?
· What's on this person's mind? What are his or her worries and fears?
· What needs might this person verbalize to others?
· What burdens did this person carry with them into church?

Ten Moments of Truth for Guests to a Church (From the video "What Visitors See.")

1. Receiving an _____ to church
2. Driving by the church _____
3. Walking to the _____
4. Entering the _____
5. Meeting _____
6. Experiencing _____ and _____
7. Entering the _____
8. Participating in the _____
9. Exiting the _____
10. Contacting people the _____

Why people don't come back to a church:

1. Cliques
2. Poorly maintained facilities
3. Tension within the congregation
4. Class and cultural distinctions
5. Poor attitude toward newcomers

Why people return to a church:

1. Everyone is involved in the welcoming - The most gratifying welcome a visitor can receive is from someone s/he wouldn't expect to welcome him/her, in a place s/he didn't expect it to happen.
2. Newcomers are acknowledged and welcomed by someone on the altar during the Mass.
3. Opportunities for newcomers to connect with established parishioners outside of weekend Mass.

4. Follow up with a phone call or visit in the week following.

Parish Process for Discerning and Implementing a Welcoming Program
1.   Identify and Form Parish Teams. These teams would be composed of people of prayer with a demonstrated commitment to the future of the Church.
    a.   Determine   decision-making   process: majority   vote, consensus, unanimous, pastor decide.
    b.   Assign   Tasks: Communications,   assessment,   and implementation.
    c.   Develop communication plan so that this process is transparent to the rest of the parish. The ultimate success of this program will rise or fall on the commitment of the rest of the parish. They need to be informed, educated, and motivated through the communication plan. Communicate early and often.
    i.   What needs to be communicated? Short answer - Everything! To whom? Everyone.
       (1)   The vision - under communicating is one of the major causes of a plan failing.
       (2)   The current assessment of reality - People need to know the reason(s) behind change.
       (3)   The change plan.
       (4)   Status updates.
    ii. Steps and considerations
       (1)   Pace - the rate at which people can absorb new information.
       (2)   Personality - different learning styles
       (3)   Develop an explicit communication strategy
       (4)   Be creative - communication about change requires more than just a sermon and bulletin article - consider:
          (a) small group discussion
          (b) youth group drama
          (c) music
          (d) special newsletter(s)
          (e) creating or using an existing video
          (f) web site
       (5)   Develop a unique vocabulary which has special meaning for your parish.
       (6)   Repeat, repeat, repeat
       (7)   Seek feedback to see if the communication is getting through.

(8)   Answering questions that people have.

2. Assess the current parish reality. Determine: 1) How welcoming is the parish? 2) How important is becoming a welcoming parish to parishioners?

    a.   Survey (sample follows on next page)

    b.   Observations

    c.   Individual Interviews

    d.   Commit the assessment of the current reality to writing, as detailed as possible, and communicate to the rest of the parish.

3. Discern God's Vision for the Ideal Welcoming Program for the Parish.

    a.   Invite the Holy Spirit into all aspects of this discernment.

    b.   This is God's vision, not our own.

    c.   Only limitation here is the imagination. Do not consider people, finances, or facilities yet.

    d.   Two different approaches:

      (1) Team Process

          (a)   During this initial team training, the task of discerning God's vision will be explained and the process begun.

          (b)   The team will go away from that training with the instruction to continue discerning God's will and to seek the input of others in this discernment while continuing to take it into personal prayer.

          (c)   The team then comes together for group prayer and meditation and to write a first draft.

          (d)   The team would then seek private feedback by asking these questions about the first draft: is it clear? Is it comprehensive? Is it compelling?

          (e)   Out of this feedback would come a revise second draft.

          (f)   The team would then obtain additional private feedback. There are four major questions the team needs to have answered about the revised second draft: what is overall reaction? Any questions about the meaning of the vision? Any ideas that need to be added or deleted? Are there better ways to express the same meaning?

          (g)   A final meeting would be held where the team would obtain a group consensus (or whatever decision making style the team has chosen) about the final form of the vision statement.

Welcoming Parish Survey

The following are some statements which will help us to determine how welcoming we are as a parish to newcomers. In order for this to be effective, please be honest. Don't answer according to the way you wish it would be, but evaluate reality as it actually exists today. First evaluate how the church is doing on a scale of 1 to 5, with 1 being great and 5 being poorly. Then evaluate each of the statements in terms of how important they are to you as a parishioner at this church, again on a scale of 1 to 5, with 1 being important and 5 being not important at all. Please circle the appropriate number. Thank you for taking the time to complete this survey.

	How is Our Church Doing?					How Important this is to you?				
Parishioners welcome the new people and try to make them feel at home.	Great 1	2	3	4	Poorly 5	Important 1	2	3	4	Not Important 5
The staff welcomes new people and tries to make them feel at home.	Great 1	2	3	4	Poorly 5	Important 1	2	3	4	Not Important 5
New people are acknowledged and/or addressed in some way during each liturgy.	Great 1	2	3	4	Poorly 5	Important 1	2	3	4	Not Important 5
Welcoming new people requires some level of comfort with changing group dynamics. Our church is comfortable with this kind of change.	Great 1	2	3	4	Poorly 5	Important 1	2	3	4	Not Important 5
We are OK with the pastor and staff focusing their attention on new people, even if it means that they may have to be less attentive to long term members.	Great 1	2	3	4	Poorly 5	Important 1	2	3	4	Not Important 5
Welcoming the newcomer requires commitment. Our staff and parishioners are committed to making the stranger in our midst feel at home.	Great 1	2	3	4	Poorly 5	Important 1	2	3	4	Not Important 5
Friendly church members greet people at each major entrance prior to and after the Mass.	Great 1	2	3	4	Poorly 5	Important 1	2	3	4	Not Important 5
Our church makes a good first impression. The building and grounds are well maintained, bulletin boards are attractive with up to date information.	Great 1	2	3	4	Poorly 5	Important 1	2	3	4	Not Important 5
Our bulletin welcomes new people and directs them to someone for further information.	Great 1	2	3	4	Poorly 5	Important 1	2	3	4	Not Important 5

	How is Our Church Doing?	How Important this is to you?
When I was a newcomer to this church, I was made to feel welcomed.	Great Poorly 1 2 3 4 5	Important Not Important 1 2 3 4 5
Our church has a written program in place for welcoming newcomers.	Great Poorly 1 2 3 4 5	Important Not Important 1 2 3 4 5
Our church has an active welcoming committee.	Great Poorly 1 2 3 4 5	Important Not Important 1 2 3 4 5
Newcomers are linked with long standing church members with whom they have something in common.	Great Poorly 1 2 3 4 5	Important Not Important 1 2 3 4 5
Our church has an active evangelism program designed to reach out to the unchurched or inactive Catholics.	Great Poorly 1 2 3 4 5	Important Not Important 1 2 3 4 5
Our church is handicap accessible.	Great Poorly 1 2 3 4 5	Important Not Important 1 2 3 4 5
Our parish truly values new parishioners	Great Poorly 1 2 3 4 5	Important Not Important 1 2 3 4 5
How long have you been a member of this parish?	_____yrs _____months	
In what year were you born?	_____	
Gender	_____Male _____Female	
Marital Status	_____Single _____Married _____Divorced _____Widowed	
What one change would you like to see our church make in order to welcome people better? (Write answer below)	Would you like to be part of a new effort to make new people feel welcomed to our church? _____Yes _____ Name _____ Contact Info _____No _____Need more information	

Thank you for completing this survey!

(2) Parish Community Process - This process is the same as the above process except that at step #6, the team would then obtain public feedback by holding a town hall type meeting, properly advertised to the entire parish. There are four major questions the team needs to have answered in this public forum: what is overall reaction? Any questions about the meaning of the vision? Any ideas that need to be added or deleted? Are there better ways to express the same meaning? The balance of the steps are the same as well.

e.   Commit the ideal to writing, as detailed as possible, and communicate to the rest of the parish.

4.   Develop a plan for moving the parish from the current reality to the ideal.

5.   Implement the plan developed. Conduct spot measurement as the plan is implemented.

6.   When plan has been fully implemented for a few months, conduct another full assessment (as in #3) to determine if ideal has been achieved.

Closing Prayer

Before the feast of Passover, Jesus knew that his hour had come to pass from this world to the Father. He loved his own in the world and he loved them to the end.

The devil had already induced Judas, son of Simon the Iscariot, to hand him over. So, during supper, fully aware that the Father had put everything into his power and that he had come from God and was returning to God, he rose from supper and took off his outer garments. He took a towel and tied it around his waist. Then he poured water into a basin and began to wash the disciples' feet and dry them with the towel around his waist.

So when he had washed their feet (and) put his garments back on and reclined at table again, he said to them, "Do you realize what I have done for you? You call me 'teacher' and 'master,' and rightly so, for indeed I am. If I, therefore, the master and teacher, have washed your feet, you ought to wash one another's feet. I have given you a model to follow, so that as I have done for you, you should also do. (Jn 13:1-15)

Observation worksheet

View to the world outside the church's neighborhood

1.   Newcomers to this community can easily find out about the church through:

a. a listing in the Yellow Pages

b. a weekly ad in the local newspaper

c. brochures in motels

d. a web site with up to date information

e. a message on the church's answering machine that lists the times of Masses.

2. The building is easy to find.

3. Anything posted outside of the church that welcomes newcomers and/or visitors?

4. Anything posted in the narthex that welcomes newcomers and/or visitors?

5. There is a prominent sign listing the church's name and times of services; the information is up to date.

First Impressions

6. The grounds are well maintained.

7. There is adequate parking, and the lot does not have major problems.

8. The building is accessible to the physically handicapped.

9. Bulletin boards or other displays inside the church are attractive and up to date.

10. The bulletin is easy to read. It lists the church's name, address, and phone number.

11. The bulletin mention newcomers or visitors

12. Are there "side doors" (non-liturgical entry points to the church community for newcomers) to the church mentioned in the bulletin or during the Mass or posted on bulletin boards?

Reinforcement

13. Each visitor is sent a letter (personally signed), called and/or visited as soon as possible.

14. The church offers special study groups (such as RCIA) for newer people.

15. The church offers several short-term groups or activities.

Worship Experience

16. Friendly members greet people at each major entrance.

17. I was welcomed through word or eye contact by the person next to me as I entered the pew

18. The priest or lector welcomed newcomers during their introductory comments

19. Newcomers were recognized and identified during the course of the Mass

20. Newcomers were personally greeted by other parishioners during the course of the Mass

21. At the Sign of Peace, I felt sincerely welcomed or greeted by the people near me

22. After Mass, there was an opportunity for me to meet other people, ie. coffee and donuts.

    a. During this social time, I was welcomed and greeted by at least one parishioner

    b. During this social time, I was included in at least one interesting conversation

    c. During this social time, I was introduced to at least one other parishioner

23. I was invited to come back

24. I was invited to come to parish activities other than Mass

25. I was introduced to the pastor, an associate pastor, or another staff person

26. I felt truly welcomed and would look forward to attending this church again

27. Childcare is available. Room numbers and directions are clearly visible.

28. The words to hymns, whether printed or displayed, are easy to read. Directions are given for all portions of the service in which people participate, such as prayers and responsive readings.

29. During the service, traditions or approaches that might be unfamiliar to people, such as the way Communion is handled, are explained.

30. Children are welcomed through special music or children's sermons, or are provided with a children's service.

31. How did the greeter respond when I identified myself as a newcomer?

32. How did the staff member respond when I identified myself as a newcomer?

Best Practices in Church Welcoming Programs

1. Top down training of Diocesan personnel, parish staffs, and parishioners designed to build awareness and to challenge communities to become more welcoming.

2. Hiring a "Welcoming the Stranger" coordinator.

3. Developing and distributing a resources book on "Welcoming the Stranger."

4. Conduct a self study and develop a three year plan for creating welcoming parishes.

5. Produced a cookbook with recipes that came from new people.

6. Produced and show a video on the importance of welcoming the stranger.

7. Parishes provide transportation to and from liturgical services for the newcomers.

8. Ask someone from outside your church community to come to all the weekend liturgies and to reflect back on the extent to which they felt (or did not feel) welcomed.

9. Newcomers are acknowledged and welcomed by someone on the altar during the Mass.

10. Everyone is involved in the welcoming of newcomers - Sometimes the most gratifying welcome a visitor can receive is from someone s/he wouldn't expect to welcome him/her, in a place s/he didn't expect it to happen.

11. Have a "welcome to the church" gathering with both newcomers and established parishioners attending.

12. After an appropriate length of time to become acquainted, invite the newcomer to commit to some parish service/ministry. Challenge the newcomer to envision what they would like to experience spiritually over the next 12 months, and then to imagine how the church can help them to realize that dream.

13. Provide visitor information cards and ask new people to either drop them in the collection basket or another designated receptacle in the church.

14. Create a Rapid Response Team. Have a group of parishioners who are willing to visit the newcomers with some fresh baked bread or cookies in the week following the newcomer's first visit to the church. Two weeks later is already too late in many cases.

15. Pray (publicly and privately) for the newcomers and for the next stranger to walk through the doors of the church. If the parish has organized prayer groups or small Christian communities, make sure they are praying for the newcomers.

16. Establish a "three-minute rule," that is, regular attendees and members spend the first three minutes after Mass visiting with someone they don't know.

17. Create a "Welcome New Members" board in the church vestibule. For each new person, there is a picture and a brief bio: where they are from, how long they've attended the church, their family, hobbies, and so on.

18. Establish programs and/or activities for the newcomer that follows up on the initial welcome. These could include: divorce recovery workshops, bereavement groups, marriage and parenting enrichment programs, out of work support and networking groups.

19. Make "Welcoming the Stranger in Our Midst" an ongoing part of every parish meeting agenda.

20. Recruit people to become umbrella escorts who would arrive half hour early on rainy days and escort people from their cars to the church on rainy days.

21. Designate well marked "Visitor Parking" spaces close to the church building and ask "regulars" to please refrain from parking there.

22. Have monthly (or quarterly depending on numbers of new people) hor'dourves gatherings of newcomers with the pastor and other parish staff.

23. No matter how efficient and cost effective an answering machine may be, newcomers are most impressed when the phone is answered by a knowledgeable, friendly, helpful person.

24. One church in Anchorage, Alaska assigns a deacon to a person or family who attends Mass for several Sundays.

25. Enfoldment Coordinators. They link visitors with a "first friend," who visits the new persons at their home. The "first friend" learns the visitors' interests and refers their names to the appropriate ministry area.

26. Integration Czar. When a person expresses interest in a program or ministry, the czar assigns a specific leader to extend an invitation to the newcomer. The czar then follows up with the leader, asking about the newcomer's response. This ensures all invitations get made.

27. Family Mentor. Assign a mentor family to each new person or family. The church attempts to match the backgrounds and interests of its mentor family with those of the newcomers. To gauge the effectiveness of the mentor program and to identify needs, a committee tracks people's attendance in Mass, involvement in service, and giving habits.

28. Tracking Changes. One church puts its people on notice: "If we don't see you, we'll call you." It tracks attendance and focuses on changes in a person's attendance pattern. A call or visit is made when someone's pattern changes.

29. Hold a parish mission designed to instruct and inspire your parishioners to become a more welcoming community. Ideal missions will: help parishioners to get in touch with God's blessings upon their lives, explain that the way to demonstrate our gratitude for these gifts is to welcome the stranger in our midst, and to instruct in the ways of being hospitable to newcomers. The Center for Parish Hospitality can provide inspirational presenters to lead your parish mission. Refer to www.catholichospitality.com/serv07.htm for further information.

Church Welcoming
Program -
Selected Bibliography

Am, W. (1990). The Church Growth Ratio Book: How to Have a Revitalized, Healthy, Growing, Loving Church. Monrovia, CA: Church Growth.

Am, Win, Carroll Nyquist, Charles Am. (1986). Who Cares about Love? How to Bring Together the Great Commission and the Great Commandment. Pasadena, CA: Church Growth.

Barna, G. (1991). User Friendly Churches. Ventura: Regal Books.

Benson, P. (1990). The Troubled Journey. Minneapolis: Search Institute.

Bernhard, Fred and Stephen Clapp. (2004). Widening the Welcome of Your Church: Biblical Hospitality and the Vital Congregation. Fort Wayne: Lifequest.

Bontrager, E. (2003). Building a Multicultural Congregation. Fort Wayne: Lifequest and New Life Ministries.

Church Growth Network. (n.d.). How to Assimilate Newcomers into Your Church. Monrovia, CA.

Clapp, S. (2004). One Hundred Ways to Reach Young Singles, Couples, and Families. Fort Wayne: Lifequest.

Clapp, S. (1994). Overcoming Barriers to Church Growth. Elgin: The Andrews Center.

Clapp, Steve and Fred Bernhard. (2002). Hospitality: Life in a Time of Fear. Fort Wayne: Lifequest.

Clapp, Steve and Fred Bernhard. (2003). Worship and Hispitality. Fort Wayne: LifeQuest.

Comiskey, J. A. (2004). The Ministry of Hospitality. Collegeville: Liturgical Press.

Delatte, P. (1921). Commentary on the Rule of St. Benedict. London: Burns and Oates.

Flavil R. Yeakley, J. (1986). Why Churches Grow (3rd ed.). Nashville: Christian Communications.

Gainsbrugh, J. (1993). Winning the Backdoor War: Growing Your Church by Closing Its Seven Backdoors. Elkgrove, CA.

Gallup, George and D. Michael Lindsay. (2002). The Gallup Guide: Reality Check for 21st Century Churches. Princeton: Gallup Orginization.

Gibson, R. B. (2005). A Companion Guide to Radical Hospitality. Maine: Paraclete Press.

Halverson, D. T. (1999). The Gift of Hospitality: In Church, in the Home, in All of Life. Atlanta: Chalice Press.

Harre, A. F. (1984). Close the Backdoor: Ways to Create a Caring Congregational Fellowship. St. Louis: Concordia.

Hershberger, M. (1999). A Christian View of Hospitality. Scottsdale, PA: Herald Press.

Homan, Daniel and Lonni Collins Pratt. (2005). Radical Hospitality: Benedict's Way of Love. Maine: Paraclete Press.

Jarvis, T. (2007). Everyday Hospitality: Simple Steps to Cultivate a Welcoming Heart. Norte Dame: Ave Maria Press.

Keifert, P. R. (1992). Welcoming the Stranger: A Public Theology of Worship and Evangelism. Minneapolis: Fortress.

Lawless, C. (2005). Membership Matters. Grand Rapids: Zondervan.

Logan, Robert E. and Larry Short. (1994). Mobilizing for Compassion. Grand Rapids: Revell.

Mann, A. B. (1983). Incorporation of New Members in the Episcopal Church: A Manual for Clergy and Lay Leaders. Philadelphia: Ascension Press.

McIntosh, G. L. (2006). Beyond the First Visit: The Complete Guide to Connecting Guests to Your Church. Grand Rapids: Baker.

McIntosh, G. (n.d.). What Visitor's See. Temecula, CA, Available from Church Growth Network.

Mead, L. B. (1993). More Than Numbers: The Ways Churches Grow. Bethesda, MD: The Alban Institute.

Merton, T. (1960). Wisdom of the Desert. Chicago: New Direction Books.

Newman, E. (2007). Untamed Hospitality: Welcoming God and Othyer Strangers. Grand Rapids: Brazos Press.

Oswald, R. M. (1992). Making Your Church More Inviting: A Step by Step Guide for In-Church Training. Washington, DC: The Alban Institute.

Oswald, Roy M. and Speed B. Leas. (1987). The Inviting Church: A Study of New Member Assimilation. Washington, DC: The Alban Institute.

Pohl, C. D. (1999). Making Room: Recovering Hospitality as a Christian Tradition. Grand Rapids: Eerdmans Publishing.

Reeves, Daniel R. and Ron Jensen. (1984). Always Advancing. San Bernardino: Here's Life Publishers.

Schaller, L. E. (1971). Assimilating New Members. Nashville: Abington.

Schroeder, A. (1997). Welcome to Our Church; A Handbook for Greeters and Ushers. St. Louis: Concordia.

Stevens, Tim and Tony Morgan. (2005). Simply Strategic Growth: Attracting a Crowd to Your Church. Loveland, CO: Group.

Stevens, Tim and Tony Morgan. (2005). Simply Strategic Volunteers: Empowering People for Ministry. Loveland, CO: Group.

USCCB. (1992). Go and Make Disciples: A National plan and Strategy for Catholic Evangelization in the United States. Washington, DC: USCCB.

USCCB. (1999). Our Hearts Were Burning Witin Us; A Pastoral Plan for Adult Faith Formation in the United States. Washington, DC: USCCB.

USCCB. (2002). Stewardship: A Disciple's Response. Washington, DC: USCCB.

USCCB. (2000). Welcoming the Stranger Among Us: Unity in Diversity. Washington, DC: USCCB.

Waltz, M. L. (2005). First Impressions; Creating Wow Experiences in your Chruch. Loveland, CO: Group.

Weeks, A. D. (1992). Welcome! Tools and Techniques for New Members Ministry. Washington, DC: The Alban Institute.

Wilson, M. (1983). How to Mobilize Church Volunteers. Minneapolis: Augburg.

About the Author

Dr. Richard McCorry is a nationally renowned presenter and the author of "Dancing with Change, A Spiritual Response to Changes in the Church," published in 2004. He is the founder of The Center for Parish Hospitality. Recently featured in St. Anthony's Messenger Magazine, Dr. McCorry travels the country, working with parishes and dioceses, helping them to develop spiritual approaches to changes in the church and has done this work for over a decade. Prior to doing this, he was the senior ministry associate for St. Pius Tenth Church in Chili, NY. He has also served as director of pastoral care for the Roman Catholic Community of the 19th Ward in the City of Rochester, a cluster of three inner city parishes. He has served as pastoral associate for the Church of the Nativity of the Blessed Virgin Mary in Brockport, NY, as campus minister for the State University of New York in Brockport, and worked in the Diocesan tribunal and pastoral planning department for several years. Richard received a Bachelor of Science degree in 1992 from St. John Fisher College majoring in philosophy and religious studies. In 1998, he obtained his Master of Divinity degree from St. Bernard's Institute. He has also earned a Master of Science degree in organizational management from Roberts Wesleyan College in 1999. In 2004 he obtained a doctor of ministry degree in transformative leadership from Colgate Rochester Crozer Divinity School.

About The Center for Parish Hospitality

The Center is dedicated to helping parishes and dioceses reclaim our rich Catholic tradition of welcoming the stranger. Guided by Scripture, prayer, Church documents, and effective organizational change principles, The Center has developed and tested a proven process for creating more welcoming parishes. Most of this process can be implemented with little outside assistance but the Center stands ready to support a parish or diocesan effort in any way necessary. Please refer to www.catholichospitality.com for further information and on line resources.

LaVergne, TN USA
05 December 2009

166076LV00002B/101/P